ISBN 0-9657828-4-0

Special Thanks to
Kelly Hillier, my life partner,
for all of her support.

TABLE OF CONTENTS

ABOUT THE AUTHOR

Craig Hillier

Craig has been speaking to teens since 1990 and speaks to over 75,000 young people each year. His high energy programs and contagious enthusiasm captivate audiences throughout the United States. In addition to leadership keynotes and school assemblies, he focuses his efforts on student leadership training. His one to three day program is a hands-on approach for today's student leader. Craig was awarded the Outstanding Young Alumni Award from Mankato State University. Craig has earned the CSP designation (Certified Speaking Professional) through the National Speakers Association. Only 5% of the 3500 members have earned this designation. He resides in Lakeville, Minnesota with his wife, Kelly and his two children, Derrick and Abigayle.

Winning Edge Seminars

20712 Jutland Place • Lakeville, MN 55044

(952) 985-5885 • (800) 446-3343 • fax (952) 985-5886

e-mail: craig@craighillier.com

www.craighillier.com

WHY SHOULD YOU READ THIS BOOK?

If you've picked up this book, you are obviously a person who strives for excellence. You may have set uncommon goals and are looking for ways to make those goals a reality. **How to Step Up as a Teen Leader *and still keep your friends*** is designed for today's young leader. It is filled with strategies to help you become your best whether you are currently in a leadership role or are interested in becoming a leader.

If you are searching to. . .

* Discover usable, hands-on ideas and techniques and to improve your leadership skills ...

* Understand the power of teen leadership...

* Gain an edge in today's competitive world...

* Take on a leadership role and still keep your friends....

THIS BOOK IS FOR YOU!

Because the average busy hard-working teen has little time to read, the book is divided into small chunks. Each chapter can be read in 15 to 20 minutes. It is designed to be entertaining and educating. This is your moment! Take advantage of this information and let's get started!

A CALL FOR LEADERSHIP

Today, you can't read a newspaper, watch TV or listen to the radio without someone asking us to make a "positive" change in our world. Most of these pleas are challenging people to make a difference in their schools, businesses and communities. The messages are often directed toward "leaders"—leaders of **all** ages. Today more than ever, young people are being challenged to make positive contributions to society. Some young people are willing to accept the leadership challenge by dedicating themselves to helping others grow as human beings. Still, there are those who are not quite sure if they have what it takes to be a leader or the desire to become one. The question is... **To Lead or Not to Lead?**

Thousands of young people are asking questions about leadership. Their questions may include, "me, a leader?" "No way!" "What is it all about?" "Is it worth the effort?" "Will I lose my friends if I step up to a leadership role?" Before a person chooses to become a leader, it is important to answer a simple question.

WHAT IS A LEADER?

There are several ways to answer this question. Some people say a leader is the person in charge of an organization or a particular event. Others say a leader is someone who believes in themselves. Some say it's a person who is admired by their peers. All these answers are correct to some degree.

If we **really** answer this question, **a leader is an individual who influences others and is willing to work and serve to make a difference.** Leaders come in all forms. Most people have the ability to lead. Still, many are mystified about the whole idea of leadership, and for good reason. There are several myths about being a leader.

One popular myth about leadership is that **leaders are people who are in charge and tell every one else what to do, then they sit back and watch things happen.** Then they take credit for what others have done. Guess what? That's not leadership; that's dictatorship.

Effective leaders do not tell others what to do; they work with everyone else to make a difference. Because effective leaders understand the power of delegation, they may not always be involved in the day to day responsibilities of a project. Often times leaders may spend their time motivating the team to stay on task and reach new heights others thought were impossible.

Leaders are born is another common myth about leadership. Could you imagine a mother giving birth and the doctor saying, "Congratulations, she's a leader!" Of course not. Some qualities and skills leaders have are innate but the vast majority are developed. Almost all the essential ingredients a person needs to become a leader can be developed through reading, studying other leaders, and learning through personal experience.

Leaders are control freaks is a third myth some people believe about leaders. If this idea is examined closely, it is easy to see how untrue it is. The best leaders are also excellent followers. Sure, leaders want to maintain control in a given situation and they accomplish this by working with other people. Leaders cannot be successful **without** the assistance and guidance of other people. This usually means associating with or following other individuals. In addition, those individuals who are followers may then take more of a leadership role in the next situation.

The final myth some people hold onto is that **leading as a young person has no impact on future success.** Nothing could be further from the truth. If a young person is willing to sacrifice now, the window of opportunity to their future will grow into a door they will be able to walk through someday.

Being a leader is an important role and when a person is ready for that commitment, it is crucial to know what is involved in that decision. When making a conscious decision to "step up" as a leader, a person should examine the burdens and benefits. Let's face it, **being a leader does have its share of burdens.** There may be days when being a leader is difficult. Sometimes it appears it would be easier to just sit back and let others take a leadership role. The burdens of leadership must be examined.

BURDENS OF LEADERSHIP

Time is a major burden. Leadership demands an incredible amount of time. For example, occasionally situations arise when a young leader attends a workshop that takes up an entire weekend. Students are typically involved in several committees that meet before and after school for an hour or two. They are also the ones working at the fundraiser while everyone else may be participating and having fun. In addition, they also have classwork, family, and job commitments. Time is the one commodity that can't be replaced. A person can get more of almost any resource except time.

Responsibility and risk taking can also be a burden of leading. For example, assume a group of young leaders convinced their school administration to play music in the hallways in between classes. If a song is playing with some negative lyrics and people become upset by the music, the leaders have to take the blame.

Leaders have to assume responsibility for the risks they take. Taking responsibility can be a humbling event. It is easy to follow. It is a challenge to lead. Most people choose to simply follow and when the project doesn't go well, they criticize the people who took the risk. Some people choose to always be followers because the pressure of responsibility and risk taking is more than they can or want to handle.

Lack of recognition is another burden. For example, assume a group of students planned a dance as a fundraiser. Almost every student had an incredible time. How many compliments will the people who put it together hear from those who attended? Rarely will individuals take the time to say thank you. Most just walk by. At times, leadership can be a thankless job.

Other burdens could include peers' jealousy, lack of commitment from others, adult expectations, the pressure to constantly be motivated, and mistakes leaders make that seem small can be magnified by those from the outside.

After examining the negative aspects of leadership, a person may wonder why anyone would want to become a leader. Students typically step into leadership roles because they believe the benefits of leading outweigh the burdens.

BENEFITS OF LEADERSHIP

Making a difference in someone else's life is a reason many young people choose to become leaders. For instance, students who volunteer their time to become a Big Brother or Big Sister receive the personal satisfaction of helping a young person who may have very few positive role models. No dollar amount can be placed on the incredible feeling a person receives when they make someone else's world better.

Gaining valuable experience is a major benefit of leading. The skills a young person develops in school will be with them throughout their lives. Learning to work with others is a valuable experience most potential employers desire for their employees. Young people graduating from school and entering the work force may hear a potential employer say, "Your resume looks great, but what experience do you have?" A common frustration young people face is dealing with the vicious cycle of how to get experience without being given a chance. Some young people edge out the competition in an employment situation because they gained experience in various school committees or events. Those experiences could include running a successful campaign for a student leadership office, masterminding an attendance recognition program for the student body, or organizing a school fundraiser for charity. Becoming a self-starter demonstrates initiative. Employers are seeking those rare individuals who are actively making positive changes for others and themselves.

Ideas can turn into action. Seeing an idea generated by an individual or group of people actually go into effect builds pride. It's an incredible feeling seeing an idea become reality. Some ideas and projects may become traditions that last for years. In essence, these ideas can become a legacy.

Respect by peers is another reason many young people choose to become leaders. Even though a classmate may never walk up to you and actually say they want to be just like you, having people look to you in a time of need makes a person feel confident about themselves and their abilities.

Additional benefits of leading include learning to work with a variety of people, building self confidence, providing unique learning opportunities, and creating a fun atmosphere.

These are the major burdens and benefits of leading. Of course there are several more benefits and burdens that could be discussed. But for sake of time and space, let's stop with those.

At this point you may be saying, "I am not sure I have what it takes to become a leader?" **Everyone has the potential to become a leader.** Maybe you have not yet decided if becoming a leader or a more effective leader is for you. Before that decision is finalized, let's dig a little deeper into the mystery of leadership.

There are two types of leaders in our world today: positive and negative.

Negative leaders can be compared to skunks. Imagine driving down the road on a hot July day and suddenly catching the aroma of a disturbed or dead skunk. How far does a skunk's odor travel? Usually a few miles. This little rodent can literally stink up a two mile radius with its scent! Are there skunks in your school or organization? They may not be as obvious as the actual rodent, but they are everywhere. Skunks can be identified as those individuals who walk up and down the hallways wreaking negativity. They say "this school sucks," "who cares about grades," "let's get high," "we tried to do a project like that but no one gave us a chance," "no one cares about us anyway." These people are known as hallway harassers. They don't buy into anything positive, but rather they look for the negative in everything they see. We are all familiar with the skunks of the world. Unfortunately, their negativity can permeate others' thoughts. Their actions can influence other people to feel the same way. Think back to the definition of a leader.

Leaders are people who influence others and are willing to work to make a difference. Skunks *have* the ability to influence others and they *work* to make a difference but it's a **negative difference**. Skunks act to make other people feel negative about themselves or their surroundings. Because you have read this far in the book I would bet you are not a negative leader. A typical skunk would not have bothered to take the time to research ideas on how to make a positive difference. After all, they believe "the world is rotten and no one cares about anything." That sad attitude will eventually catch up with the skunk. After all, who wants to be around a person like that for an extended period of time? No one.

The positive leader can be compared to a squirrel. If you live near a wooded area, take the time to observe a squirrel. They are always busy, moving and planning for the future. They communicate with each

other and then work together until the project is done. Squirrels are not out to hurt anyone. They are out to make their situation better.

Schools and organizations are also filled with squirrels. They don't draw a lot of attention to themselves but they are always working to improve themselves and their situation. They are planning, motivating others, and getting down to work. Squirrels will succeed because they are team players determined to make a positive difference. We need more squirrels in our schools and in our world.

At this point you should have a better idea of what leadership is all about. If you are currently a leader or happen to be one of the rare individuals who is ready to step up as a leader, the rest of this book will become a valuable tool.

The book is divided into two parts. The first part outlines leadership laws. Part two examines the actual leadership skills. Keep in mind this manual is not the complete one-stop-shop on becoming a leader. Use this book as one of many tools, just like a good carpenter must have an entire tool chest filled with various tools for different jobs. Imagine how difficult it would be to build a house with just one tool. Obviously it would be impossible. This manual is just one tool in your tool chest of leadership material. It is vital to search and research ideas and strategies that allow you to grow as a leader.

Becoming a leader can be compared to high jumping. If you have never participated in the high jump, you have probably witnessed the event on television or at a track meet. Athletes set the bar at a certain height they think they can jump over. A high jumper works extremely hard at getting into peak physical shape to make it over the bar. Once they make it over the bar, the bar is immediately raised in small two inch increments. Raising it six inches at a time would be too dramatic. The small raises provide the high jumper with consistent and upward growth.

Becoming a leader is just like high jumping. Some people start at a higher level and continue to raise their standards and skills. Others who are new to leadership may start a little slower. It does not matter where you start. Just start. Leadership is not about being better than anyone else. It is about becoming your best and having the people around you do the same. This book is designed to help you become a little bit better in several areas of your life.

At the end of each chapter there will be a short exercise. I challenge you to work through the questions or exercises before moving on to the next chapter. Each exercise is designed to reinforce the material presented and allow you to implement some of the ideas into your life. **Remember, learning is not just knowing, it is doing.** By completing the exercises this material becomes yours.

EXERCISE:

1. List five or more qualities of skunk (negative) leaders.

2. List five or more qualities of squirrel (positive) leaders.

3. What characteristics do you have that will allow you to become a leader?

PART 1:

LEADERSHIP LAWS

LAW #1: 10%-80%-10%

This is probably one of the most unique chapter titles you will ever read. "What does it mean?" It is an important law all leaders must grasp. 10-80-10 is an equation successful leaders must grasp.

Whether it's an individual or team project, the 10-80-10 law will become evident. Let's start with the bottom ten percent. It does not matter who you are or how many great ideas you generate, ten percent of the people you present them to will not like the ideas. Not only that, but ten percent of the people who hear the idea do not like you in the first place! Some people won't like you because everyone else likes you. You may say, "that's not fair or right!" That may be true, but it is a fact. Why ten percent of the population will not like you is perplexing. Maybe you remind them of someone in their past they did not get along with. To them, your values and decisions may be poor. Possibly your hair style or the clothes you wear

are not appropriate in the mind of the person judging you. Maybe your culture is misunderstood and instead of taking the time to get to know you as an individual they treat you based on old worn out, misguided perceptions. There are thousands of reasons why ten percent of the population may not take a liking to you. This ten percent will have a difficult time cooperating with you and your ideas. They typically criticize you or exercise their right not to get involved with new ideas. It can be depressing to think some people will not believe in you no matter what you do. Unfortunately, that is life.

There is a flip side to the bottom ten percent. The upper ten percent of the population will take an immediate liking to you and it may not be clear why they feel that way. Have you ever noticed some people bond with you instantly? It's fascinating. People may be drawn to you for a variety of reasons. Maybe they admire your looks, the way you play sports, or how you play a particular instrument in band. It could be your sense of humor that draws others to you. Who knows, you could remind them of someone they respected in another community. For what ever reason, ten percent of the people you meet will take an immediate liking to you or your ideas. It's great to know that at least ten percent of the population is on your side right off the bat!

The middle percentage, eighty, is the most significant variable in the equation. The middle 80 percent are those individuals in the school or population who can be influenced to either side of the equation. A leader's thoughts and actions determine which side of the equation the individuals in the 80 percentile will fall. Will they lean toward the bottom ten percent and not listen or cooperate or can they be influenced to join the top ten percent who believe in you and what you stand for? Will they choose to participate in making a positive difference?

Time and energy will answer that question. Upon which percentage of people should a person concentrate their energy? **If you focus your energy trying to please the bottom ten percent, I suggest buying a big bottle of aspirin.**

Trying to focus all of your energy and pleasing the bottom ten percent is like trying to pound a nail into a board with your forehead. It doesn't work very well. All you end up doing is developing a headache and hurting yourself. One strategy for dealing with the negative criticism of the bottom ten percent is to challenge them when they are cutting you or your ideas down.

For instance, say you're planning a spirit day for the students in your school that involves a mini-Olympics. Most likely there will be at least one person who will think the idea is stupid or not worthwhile. They may make this comment to your face or behind your back. For this example, let's say they say something negative to you at lunch. You may hear, "that mini-Olympics is not going to be any fun."

Instead of getting defensive and justifying why it going to be fun, you might say, "you could be right. If you were planning the day, what would you do differently?" Watch their surprised response. One of two things will probably be said. Option number one, "Well, it's just dumb, nobody wants to do it." If they do not have an idea on improving the event, what does their comment or criticism mean to you as a leader? **Nothing!** If they can't or won't improve on the idea, they are just blowing hot air and their critical comments should be ignored.

The second option would be giving you an idea that could be used. They may say, "You should get the teachers involved." If this is a good idea, it's time to recruit that person. You may say, "That's a great idea. Would you be willing to help?" At this point you've got them. They have to put up or shut up. If they get involved, you may have designed a better day. If they don't get involved, the idea could still be used and you have made that person feel important because you took the time to listen to them.

If they are not willing to get involved in the event, they will think twice before cutting your ideas down the next time. They will soon understand if they take a cut at your ideas, they will be challenged to back up the comment. At times, the bottom ten percent can make leadership challenging.

The upper ten percent is on your side. However, if all of your focus and efforts are on the upper ten percent, it is like driving that same nail into a board with a sledge hammer. It's overkill. They are already on your side or team. Maintaining a positive relationship is vital, but it will take more than ten percent of the people to make an impact.

The 80 percent in the middle should draw most of your focus and energy. Does everyone have to like you? No, but think about it. How often do you want to be around people you don't like? Some people will not even answer the telephone if they believe someone they don't care for is calling. We constantly avoid being around those we don't like or look up to. Remember, 80 percent can be influenced. Why not try to influence as many people in the middle to take your side or join your team? It makes sense. Will everyone in the eighty percentile be influenced by you or your ideas? Probably not.

However, skilled leaders can influence the majority. If people like and trust you, creating change is much easier.

One thought to keep in mind is that percentages are not exact. Leaders understand that achieving one hundred percent agreement on any issue is close to impossible. The best leaders strive to pour their energy into people and projects that can make a positive difference.

This book is designed to illustrate strategies and skills that help a young leader develop the tools to influence a majority of the population. Leadership is about helping others achieve beyond their current boundaries or limitations. Before starting the next chapter, it's important to complete the exercise on the next page.

EXERCISE:

1. Have the ten percent who don't like you influenced you to alter your behavior? Give an example.

2. Describe five things you could do to influence the eighty percent in the middle?

3. What are the negative side affects of associating only with the upper ten percent who like and trust you?

LAW #2:

CONTRIBUTION MAKES THE DIFFERENCE

Imagine a water glass filled to the rim with water. Adding any more water to the glass would obviously make it run over, unless the law of contribution is understood. The only way to get more water into the glass is to pour some of it out, thus creating more room. This glass scenario is similar to the cycle of human growth and leadership.

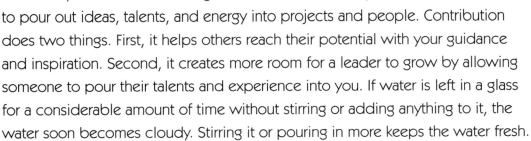

If we are going to grow as individuals we must understand the power of contributing. Leaders have the ability to pour out ideas, talents, and energy into projects and people. Contribution does two things. First, it helps others reach their potential with your guidance and inspiration. Second, it creates more room for a leader to grow by allowing someone to pour their talents and experience into you. If water is left in a glass for a considerable amount of time without stirring or adding anything to it, the water soon becomes cloudy. Stirring it or pouring in more keeps the water fresh.

Our world is becoming a very selfish place. There are so many people just looking out for themselves instead of trying to help someone else. Most people are more concerned about receiving instead of giving. Each and every day a leader has the opportunity to contribute something to almost every one they meet. Each day, a leader has the opportunity to pour encouragement into someone else's life. It may come through giving kind words, sticking up for someone who is being treated unfairly, or getting involved in a community service project.

The law of contribution stresses giving for the sake of giving. It helps us grow into better human beings. Unselfish acts of contribution build character.

A principal once shared a story with me about the power of contribution. A new student named Daryl moved into the school district. He was a polite young man who basically kept to himself. Unfortunately, his family situation was not the best. His mother was a single parent and he had three brothers and three sisters. Even though his mom had a job, the family was still on welfare. The family could not afford any luxuries. Most of the family's clothes came from the Salvation Army. The car had broken down and sat unused because they could not afford the $750 repair bill. Daryl used his bicycle to get around.

Daryl decided to get a job at a local grocery store to help the family make ends meet. Unfortunately, his only mode of transportation was his bicycle. One frigid February winter evening, he was riding his bicycle into town and realized he was running late for work. Daryl increased his speed and as he approached a stop sign, he decided to run it to save some time. When he was in the middle of the intersection a car collided with him, causing him to be thrown from the bike. The car did not stop to see if he was alright and sped off from the scene of the accident. Miraculously, Daryl made it to work that evening with only a sprained knee. The bicycle was destroyed.

One of Daryl's classmates heard about the accident. The next day in school she decided to do something to help. She started a voluntary groundswell with her fellow students. She would approach a student, tell them what happened to Daryl, and ask for a small donation. Her goal was to raise $40 to replace his used bicycle with another used bicycle that could be purchased at a local thrift shop.

During a Friday afternoon pep rally, she asked Daryl to come forward. Another student who had helped her raise money rolled out a bicycle. However, the bicycle was not a used one. It was a brand new mountain bicycle purchased for $175.

As the principal shared the story with me he said, "you should have seen the look in Daryl's eyes as they rolled the bicycle out and told him it was his. He just stared in disbelief. There was not a dry eye in the gymnasium."

As he shared the story, I thought— how incredible! Here was a young leader committed to making a difference. She was a full time leader and understood the law of contribution. She was not concerned about getting her picture in the community paper or school yearbook. She did not expect extra credit from a teacher. She just wanted to help someone out of a difficult situation. Instead of just thinking about it, she took action. That is what leadership can do.

What could you do to contribute? Maybe it is something big like a city-wide fundraiser. Maybe it is something small like helping someone with their homework. It is not just what you are doing for them, it is what you are doing for yourself. As mentioned earlier, when you give back, pride and character are built. It helps you appreciate what you have. It seems there are too many people just looking out for themselves and who have a need for personal recognition. If you are always concerned about your problems, you will always have them. When you concentrate on helping others solve their problems, it is amazing how people start helping you solve your own problems. Full-time leaders live all year around by the Christmastime theme, "It is better to give than to receive."

It all boils down to caring. If you are serious about really making a difference in your school or community consider the C.A.R.E. method (see the following page). If a person commits to the C.A.R.E. method, they will see a ripple effect with their peers. Leaders do not wait for someone else to start the wave. They throw the first pebble into the pond and start to shake things up in a positive way.

WHO CARES?

Every day of my life I am committed to making a positive difference.
I realize my actions affect everyone around me.
Therefore, my thoughts and actions will lead others to a new height.
The world will be a better place because 'I C.A.R.E.'

Compliment at least three people a day.

Act in others' best interests.

Respect the differences in others.

Extend a helping hand.

_____   _____

Signature   Date

EXERCISE:

The following are daily questions to ask yourself before you go to sleep at night.

1. How did I grow as a person today?

2. How did I make the world a better place?

3. Can you describe a time when someone contributed to your life without expecting anything in return? Explain.

4. How did that make you feel?

5. What talent or skill have you developed that you could "pour" into someone else's life?

LAW #3:

CHANGE: MOVE WITH IT OR IT MOVES YOU.

Let's take a journey back in time. It's Christmas 1977. My brother, sister and I have just completed the traditional activity of opening presents. Then, my father brought this huge wrapped box out from the closet. The tag was labeled with all three of our names: Craig, Chris, and Cindy.

"What is it?" I remember shouting. "You'll just have to find out for yourself," my father said. He no more than set it down and we opened it like three savages. I couldn't believe it. I was shocked! It was our very own home video arcade game. There would be no need to waste quarters at the arcade anymore. Yes, we had our very own Pong game. For those of you too young to remember this home entertainment system, I will enlighten you. Pong featured three state of the art games. The first game was creatively called "Pong." Basically, it was like playing tennis with two people. Each player had a control stick with a round knob that controlled the rectangular block representing a tennis racquet. A blip of light representing a ball would go back and forth on the television screen. The object of the game was to get

the blip past your opponent. WOW! The second game was called "Super Pong." It was basically the same game with smaller blocks for each player and a faster blip of light. If a person wanted to play a game all by themselves, they could play hand ball. This game featured one rectangular block and one slow blip that would bounce off of a wall. The object of the game was to see how long you could keep the ball in place.

When I share that story with a group of students, most of them laugh. "Boring!" "That's all the game did?" are a few of the comments I hear. Most young people would rather watch two people fish than play that game. When you compare the old Pong system to the video games of today and the games of the future, it's no wonder watching people fish becomes an option. The games of today are better because they are more sophisticated.

Most people like the change. **The people who don't like change are those who are stuck in their old ways. Some people can't make adjustments to new or different ways of thinking.**

To illustrate this point fold your hands the way you normally fold them. Take note which thumb is over which thumb and how your fingers are interlocked. Now,

reverse the way you cross your hands. If your right thumb was over your left thumb, put your left thumb over your right thumb and reverse the way your fingers are interlocked. If your left thumb was over the right thumb, do the exact opposite. How does that feel? Most people say it's awkward and does not feel right. Why? Because it was probably the first attempt to change something that has been automatic for years. If you were to practice reversing your  hands twenty times the change would soon become more comfortable. It's that flexibility that will allow today's youth to be successful in the years to come. Change is inevitable.

Adapting to rapid change is one advantage young people have today. Most young people like and encourage it. If there is a new gadget, tool, or game in the world that's better, stronger, or faster, young people want it. Most young people are willing to try something new even if they are not mastering it immediately. Persistence and flexibility will lead to personal growth.

Have you ever heard the phrase, "if you do not move with change, it will move you?" If a person becomes stuck in their old ways, change will move them. Chances are it could move them out of their career. If an individual cannot adapt to change and adapt their skills to the current times, they, too, will become a dinosaur.

Look at the recording industry as an example. Your parents used to buy vinyl records, 8-track tapes or cassette tapes. Suddenly, the compact disc has revolutionized the way people listen to music. The first CDs started showing up in 1984. The record companies thought it was a short  lived fad so they continued to make records and discarded the possibility of CDs taking over. Four short years later there was not a record factory in business! What if you only had the one skill of making records? You are out of a job. It's been forecasted that today's teens will have seven to eight different careers by the time they retire. The successful leader keeps their vision to the future wide open. They anticipate the future and make adjustments or change at an opportune time; they don't wait for someone else to make the change for them. If you wait for someone else to make the change, chances are you will end up with the short end of the stick.

People usually have a difficult time adapting to change because of several fears. One fear about change is not knowing if the change will be beneficial. The famous phrase, "if it's not broke, why fix it?" causes people to stay in only one mode of thinking. Maybe it's broke but they have not figured that out yet.

Another fear people face when dealing with change is learning new skills. Grocery stores used to place a price sticker on each item they sold. The cashier  would manually key each grocery item at the checkout counter. The margin of error was great because it was easy to strike an inaccurate number. In addition to the possibility of error, it would take a long time to price the items and for customers to check out.

The bar code scanning system was introduced in the mid 1980's. It allowed a cashier to simply scan a grocery item across an instrument that decoded the bar code and automatically registered an accurate price. At first people were skeptical and feared learning a new cash register. After the initial fear disappeared, cashiers loved the new technology. There were fewer mistakes and they could check out more customers in a given period of time. If the scanners were taken away from the cashiers today and a store reverted back to individual sticker pricing it is easy to assume the cashiers would not be pleased. People soon forget the fear of change after they realized the benefit of adapting to it.

One additional fear people face with change is being criticized for their effort. Trying a new approach to a situation may cause others to judge you a "radical." Instead of examining the change, people believe criticizing the person making the change may cause them to stay with the current way of thinking.

Effective leaders do not fall into this trap. First, they do not criticize others who are attempting something new or profound. They keep their opinion to themselves and observe how the change is working. Second, leaders listen to the criticism of others when creating a change but believe in themselves and their ideas enough to continue until the ideas are working or a better solution is found.

Is change always good? That depends on your perspective. Some changes can be damaging. For instance, creating designer drugs that are addictive and endanger the lives of young people who take them is not a positive change. Another example of rapid change is the technology used to bring a child into the world today. Science has provided techniques to virtually guarantee the child's gender. Some people see this as a positive change while others see this technology as a negative change. Change can be good and bad. **If you can adapt to change, your chances of being successful increase dramatically.**

EXERCISE:

1. What changes have you seen in your life that have been bene-
    ficial? (example: products, philosophies or life styles.)

2. What changes have you seen in your life that have been nega-
    tive? (example: products, philosophies or life styles.)

3. Why would one person see change as negative while some-
    one else sees it positive?

Before beginning the next chapter, complete the following exercise. Place an "X" next to the action you would take.

A.   It's a hot day. You have your swimming suit on and the pool is available. Would you?

_____Dive In.

_____Check water temperature before entering.

B.   It's not dress up day at school but you have a new outfit that may be considered "dressy." Would you?

_____Wear it to school.

_____Save it and wear it at the appropriate time.

C.   A friend suggests a new restaurant that neither one of you has eaten at. Would you?

_____Try it.

_____Suggest a familiar restaurant.

D.   A new class with a new teacher has been introduced. It sounds interesting, but you are not sure. Would you?

_____Take the class.

_____Wait until the next semester to see what others have to say about it.

E.   Your car breaks down. It's a mile and a half to the repair station. Would you?

_____Hitchhike.

_____Walk.

F.   You have an opportunity to give a five minute speech or write an eight page report. Would you?

_____Give the speech.

_____Write the paper.

G.   You see someone you would like to ask out on a date. Would you?

_____Ask them directly for a date.

_____Have a friend ask for you.

H.   Someone asks you to get involved in a sports betting pool. Would you?

_____Get in.

_____Stay out.

I.   A free bungy jump is offered. Would you?

_____Take the offer.

_____Pass on the offer.

J.   A practice sign up sheet is being passed out for a sport you have never participated in but have some interest in. Your schedule would allow you to play if you chose to do so. Would you?

_____Try out.

_____Think about it and join next year.

Survey results: Total number of "X's" in the first blanks _____

Total number of "X's" in the second blanks_____

0-3   Low risk taker

4-6   Medium risk taker

7-10 High risk taker

LAW #4:

RISK- THERE IS NO REWARD WITHOUT IT.

I was visiting a friend in Denver, Colorado one day and we decided to go to the club for a workout. After I finished my exercise program, I decided to relax by the pool. As I found an empty beach chair, I started to observe the people in and around the pool. One section of the pool was blocked off for a group of small children taking beginner swimming lessons. All but two children were in the pool. Melissa and Bobby stood by the pool's edge. I knew their names because the instructor and the children in the pool repeated their names several times trying to persuade the two to jump in the pool for the lesson with the other children. After ten minutes of this verbal torture, Bobby jumped into the water and was soon dog paddling. The class continued to try to persuade Melissa but to no avail. She did not get into the pool the entire lesson. I overheard her mother saying this was her third lesson and she had yet to enter the pool.

As I watched this event, I wondered how many people are just like Melissa? How many individuals are afraid to let go of the sure thing and jump in and see what they can accomplish? Melissa was safe and comfortable watching from the side. It was familiar territory. By letting go of familiar territory, she risked failure, embarrassment, and rejection. It seems many people are afraid to take a risk and jump into the pool of life.

Is that example right on target? Should everyone be a high risk taker? High risk takers, those who scored a seven to ten on the survey preceding this chapter, would say risking is the only way to accomplish anything important in life. But is that right for everyone? Could Melissa be better off by just watching the others?

Go back to the first question on the survey. If you marked the first response, "Dive In," it indicated taking a higher risk rather than checking out the temperature. What negative outcomes are possible if a person leaps without looking? First, there may be no water in the pool! Some people who marked that response may be saying to themselves, "Oh, I didn't think of that!" Another negative side effect may include the water being ice cold. Of course if that was the situation, the high risk taker would probably shiver and try to trick other people into jumping in. Another negative aspect of leaping without checking is that the pool could be very shallow. An injury is almost certain when diving into two feet of water. It is easy to conclude that being a high risk taker is not always the best option.

On the other hand, assume you marked, "check water temperature before entering." What negative side effects are possible in that situation? A person may take too much time getting used to the water. By the time they get in, the other people in the group are finished swimming. Deciding not to get in at all may be another negative aspect of staying on the shore. Someone may decide to wait until the water warms up or the weather is better. What if it rains or the pool is closed the next day?

What style is the best? Every situation is different. People live with a different intensity. A leader learns to evaluate each situation carefully before deciding how much to risk.

High risk takers set lofty goals and want to accomplish them in a short period of time. However, they may have to deal with an incredible amount of failure and rejection as their decisions and actions may not be thought all the way through.

Low risk takers have a different life intensity. Their goals are more realistic and may take longer to achieve. They will probably face less failure and rejection since their goals are carefully planned out. The frustration low risk takers face is the time it takes to accomplish their goals. Sometimes low risk takers miss out on their goals or opportunities because they take too much time to decide whether it is right for them or not.

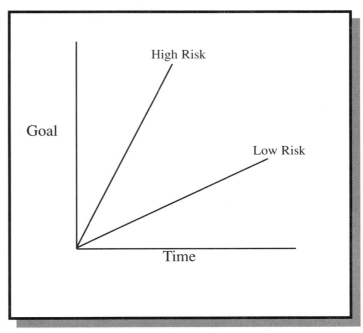

(*Inspired by Jim Cathcart, 1995 National Speakers Meeting)

Whether a person is a high risk taker or low risk taker, both styles have downfalls. High risk takers could save themselves a lot of personal pain if they would take the time to look before they leaped into a decision. It's great to have the courage to just go for it, but it is vital to have an idea of what you are jumping into. Low risk takers become more effective if they challenge themselves to make a decision that may not have a guaranteed result. Even if it takes a little more time, it's vital to get in the pool of life. Staying on the shore leads to regret in the long run. It would be a tragedy to get to the end of your life and know you could have been more successful if you were willing to take a risk that could pay off.

Learning how to take educated risks is a key to being a successful leader. Before taking a risk it may be wise to evaluate the situation by asking a few questions.

What's the worst thing that could happen?

Assume you are involved in a fundraiser that includes selling magazine subscriptions door to door. Selling in a situation like that is perceived to be a high risk activity by many people. You never know who could answer the door. However, if that is the only thought that goes through a person's mind, they will probably never knock on any doors. By asking "what's the worst thing that could happen," a person may come up with "they could reject me or slam the door in my face!" "They may not buy a magazine" could be another risk of knocking on the door. We could go on and on about the possible rejections a person could face in that situation. Those two responses are probably the most common. Asking yourself "what's the worst thing that could happen" is only one of the questions to ask. The other question to ask is, **What's the best thing that could happen?**

It's important to look at both sides of the equation. Maybe your customers have been waiting to order magazines or their subscription needs to be renewed. They may jump at the opportunity to order a magazine and help out a young person.

Can I deal with either situation? is the third question to ask before taking a risk. If the door gets slammed in your face or they do not want to place an order, is continuing on to the next house possible? Or has the rejection ruined the day? Obviously, it's easier to deal with success than failure. However, in the magazine sale example, a person will meet more people who won't buy than people who will buy. If a person can deal with failure and rejection, they are destined to accomplish incredible feats.

It's important to keep failure and rejection in the proper perspective. A person can do that by looking at failure or rejection as a learning experience. Top leaders look at failure as an opportunity to improve their skills, learn about themselves, and develop a sense of humor by learning to laugh at themselves.

> **The key to effective risk taking lies not only in your ability to deal with rejection but to eliminate as much risk as possible.**

This can be done by doing risk homework. It may be wise to find out who else has taken a similar risk. What did they do right or wrong? Who has made this risk pay off? How did they do it? What steps were followed? Is there a book or additional materials that would be beneficial to study? Instead of just leaping in without the knowledge, eliminate as much trial and error as possible by re-searching the risk before it's too late to recover from a mistake. There are rare instances when a person leaps blindly and everything turns out great. Those situations tend to be the exception, not the rule.

Look at those people in our world who have taken a risk. Colonel Sanders was an individual who took a risk. At age 65 he received his first Social Security check for $95. He made up his mind there was no way he could live on that amount of money so he decided to take a risk. He had a recipe for chicken that everyone loved. He decided to market his recipe. He entered a restaurant and asked the owner to try his recipe. "If you use the recipe, I would like a ten per-

cent royalty," the Colonel said. The restaurant owner thought he was crazy. "Get out of here, you bum," he was told. So Colonel Sanders went to the next restaurant. He faced the same response from the owner. Time and time again he faced rejection. Was this a silly risk with no reward? Finally, an owner bought into  his idea. It was restaurant owner number 1009. It took the Colonel three years to find the one owner who said yes to his opportunity. The rest is history. There are many KFC restaurants located throughout the world serving the popular recipe the Colonel created. His risk paid off.

Do all risks pay off? No. We all know people who have jumped in and lost. Effective leaders understand it is alright to risk and fail as long as a person learns from the risk. **Leaders understand failure is an event, not a person.** Life is a process of taking risks to find out what can be accomplished. One thing is certain. The success people receive is in direct proportion to their ability to take risks and live and learn from the positive and negative consequences. Keep in mind: no risk, no reward!

EXERCISE:

1. Think about a recent risk-taking situation in your life. Was the risk successful or unsuccessful?

2. Before the risk was taken did you go through a mental questionnaire? If so, what were some of the questions you asked?

3. Has the fear of failure held you back from being your best? If so, what were you afraid of?

4. What is one specific risk you could take immediately that would improve your life if it paid off?

LAW #5:

ROLE MODELING

An important philosophy leaders must grasp is that actions speak louder than words. We all know some individuals talk one message and live another. In a very short time they lose their credibility because they are not true to themselves or to those around them.

I am reminded of a personal experience. While I was in college I was a youth baseball coach during summer vacation. After my first summer of coaching, a mother approached me and said, "Craig, you had a major influence on my son." Of course that made me feel incredible to know her son looked up to me. She went on to say, "he attended every one of the high school home varsity basketball games you played."

When I was in high school it was difficult to separate me from a basketball. As a senior, I was the team captain. From ninth grade through twelfth grade my jersey number was 33 for home games. The mother went on to say that after each home game her son would come home and put his red and white jersey on. Red and white were our school colors. He took electrical tape and made a number on the tank top. You guessed it: 33. "He idolized you!" she exclaimed. "However," she went on to say, "one time it got him into a bit of trouble." There is one thing I have not told you about myself. When I work out or play sports, I get cotton mouth. The only way to relieve cotton mouth is to drink water or spit. In the middle of a game there were times when I couldn't get a drink so during a free throw I lined up on a certain side of the foul line, turned my head, and spit under a curtain that hung in the corner of the gymnasium. I never thought about it. As it turned out, this young man sat in the same corner as the curtain. He saw me do this countless times.

"During a peewee basketball tournament my son did the same thing you used to do," the mother went on to say. "He turned to spit, but he didn't look where he was spitting. It went on the referee's pant leg. He was called for a technical foul and the team ended up losing the game by one point."

I felt about two inches tall after hearing that story. Did I intentionally spit in the corner so a young man watching me would eventually do the same thing on a referee's pant leg? No! I didn't even know who this young man was at the time. But he knew who I was and he repeated my actions. As I mentioned in the introduction, it is important for leaders to watch their actions because someone you may not even know may be looking at you and your actions. When I was spitting in the corner, I wasn't aware a young kid would copy my actions.

Again, our actions speak louder than words. Young leaders need to understand there are individuals looking to them even when they don't realize it. In any given situation, a follower looks to the leader for their response and often copies their actions.

This can be positive or negative. If a leader starts something negative such as a rumor or takes part in an unhealthy choice like taking drugs, others may follow. Leaders are role models. The question is, what are you modeling? If someone adopts your beliefs, attitudes, and behaviors, will they become a better person because of it? This is an awesome and for some an overwhelming responsibility.

> **If a person wants to make a difference they have to not only deliver a message, but live the message.**

Finding a role model in today's world is not easy. However, there are individuals all of us can emulate. Many people search for role models who are professional athletes, wealthy business people, or movie stars. But there are many leaders who may not be famous but who are making a difference in our communities and world. In many cases, parents are excellent role models. A great deal of a person's attitudes and actions come from their parents.

Most coaches and teachers are also great role models. Many of them have dedicated their lives to helping others to help themselves. Despite not being paid well, they have chosen to dedicate their lives to making a positive impact on young people.

Are all parents, teachers, and coaches excellent role models? Absolutely not! However, we can learn from all their examples. If someone is modeling a negative behavior, we can mentally commit to never adopting their actions.

If you are fortunate to find a role model in life, it may be wise to avoid idolizing them as if they were a god. Everyone is human. Everyone can make a mistake. If you put someone on a pedestal and they fall off because of a bad decision, it may put you in a difficult position.

Someone once told me, "It is great to want to be like somebody, but remember to be yourself or you will become a fake." If leaders identify a few role models and then become their own role models, the world would become a better place.

EXERCISE:

1. Who have you tried to model your beliefs, attitudes, and behaviors after?

   Why?

2. How has that helped or hurt you in your life?

3. List five role models who have lost their reputation. How did this change make you feel?

4. Identify three personal characteristics that would make you a good role model.

PART 2:

"TIONS"
OF
LEADING

ASSOCIATION

Have you ever been in a situation when you were involved in a competition with someone who was more skilled than you were? What happened? Did you do better or worse? Usually a team or an individual raises their effort and performs at a higher caliber in order to compete. What if you compete against someone who is not as skilled as you or your team? Have you ever performed poorly because the competition was perceived as weak or inferior? Most people have. People usually perform to the level of their competition.

 This can be illustrated by the game of golf. I love the game, but my scores do not show it. The biggest challenge I have is consistency. I am consistently inconsistent. There are times when my game is awesome and I feel unstoppable. Other days, I shake my head and wonder why I even play the game.

I realized my scores were lower when the person I played with was better than I was. My competitive nature caused me to concentrate deeper and focus more on my practice swings.

On the other hand, when paired with a beginner my concentration was not as strong because my competitive nature was not challenged. There are several valuable lessons to be gained by this example. One of them includes playing against myself even if the competition is not very strong. Second, I must continue to challenge myself by playing with people who have more skills than I do. As we will discuss in the chapter on education, we can learn a great deal from those who have honed their skills.

In addition to competition, have you ever associated with a group of people who developed a habit you did not originally have but soon developed? May-

be the group used a particular word or phrase and soon you started saying the same word. Or maybe they dressed with a certain style of clothes and suddenly that style became your style. Maybe a friend moved to a certain part of the county and when they returned for a visit three years later their speech patterns were different. Not only do we perform to the level of our competition, but we start to become like the people

around us. The question is, do the people you associate with drive you to a new height or destroy you? Do they make you better than you were because they challenge you or do they drag you down? Have the adopted habits from your friends made you healthier or could they cause long term problems?

I have received several letters from young people regarding association. One letter told of a young man who earned an all-conference status as a running back on the football team. During the summer he started to hang around a group of people who were not athletes. This group referred to themselves as the "brew crew." They got their kicks out of getting drunk and smoking mari-juana. It wasn't long before this young man took up the group's habit. When it was time to start summer football practice he chose not to go out. Keep in mind he was an all-conference player the year before. His association with his friends led him to believe football was not all that important. "Being a part of a real team like the brew crew was a lot more important than playing a stupid sport like football," was repeated several times by his new friends.

Unfortunately, the letter stated that his high school football team lost in the state finals. They lost because the person who took his position had very little experi-ence at the varsity level. He went on to say, "it was a sad day when I realized I would never get a chance to play in the state finals again." He had dreams about being on a championship team since he was in grade school. He concluded, "I wish I never would have started hanging out with the brew crew. Who knows what would have happened if I would have gone out for the team and remained drug free." His association ended up hurting him more than helping him.

On the positive side of association, another young man told me he knew nothing about wrestling but had always wanted to try out for the team. A good friend of his was a star wrestler. Through some persuasion from his friend, the young man tried out. His freshman year he was on the B-squad. He continued to wrestle his friend who was more experienced and weighed more. He started to make dramatic improvements. He was willing to stretch himself. At the end of his junior year he made it to the sectional finals. His goal for his senior year was to make it to the state tournament. If this young man would not have stretched himself by competing against better skilled wrestlers, he probably would not have reached his success level, section champ. His positive association took him to a height he could not have achieved by himself.

Understanding how associations work is vital information for leaders to understand. No one can tell you who your friends should be. However, it is important to evaluate your associations. If you hang out with people who are constantly negative, gossip behind people's backs, or use drugs or alcohol, it may be wise to reevaluate those relationships. **Remember, we become like the people we associate with.**

Effective leaders associate with people who have the same desire to succeed. They associate with a variety of people who have different talents. In other words, leaders seek friendships that are mutually beneficial. These friendships become valuable when something they are not knowledgeable about confronts them. For instance, a leader takes on a new project involving a fundraiser. The project calls for a team of four people to spearhead the project. For this example, let's assume the leader is a great promotion person. They are creative and have strength in designing materials that get people excited about a new project. Fantastic, but that person may have several areas of lesser ability which might include accounting, project planning, or working with the administration. Instead of being an ego maniac and try to complete the project by themselves, they seek out people who are competent in those areas that they are not. The association allows the team to be stronger together than it would be with just one individual doing all the work. The best associations involve people who are willing to speak their minds, express their opinions, and avoid just agreeing with everyone's ideas. Associations allow people to create a vision from a different perspective. They challenge each other by asking questions and giving suggestions. If the individuals in a group always agree with each other, there may be a problem.

The power of association is very broad. Advertisers understand the use of association in their advertising campaigns. However, when corporations use famous spokespeople in promotional campaigns, they are certainly taking a bit of a risk. If the person they employ to represent their product makes a bad life mistake, it can be a reflection of their company. Therefore, many companies are very reserved about using "stars" to represent their products.

Associations can be very valuable. Before this book was published several people in my association including my wife, students, youth speakers, advisors, and a college professor reviewed and critiqued the book before it went to press. Thank goodness. Their suggestions made me reevaluate the material and help me clarify some ideas. They offered several suggestions that improved the book and made it easier to follow.

I had to endure some criticism and understand that all the bases were not covered. The best associations challenge each member to achieve positive results. They also help me reach levels that would have been impossible to reach by myself.

EXERCISE:

1. Write down the initials of ten people that you hang out with.

2. Evaluate the association by placing a (+) sign next to the individuals who build you up and help you make good decisions. Place a (-) next to any individual who influences you to make unwise or unhealthy choices. Their influence could be based upon what they say or what they do. If an individual has little to no influence, write N/A for not affected.

3. Review your evaluations. Hopefully you have a lot of pluses. If there are minus signs it may be time to re-evaluate your relationships with these individuals. If you continue to associate with this person, become more aware about how your actions reflect their actions.

4. What additional associations could you develop that would make you a better leader? Beside their names write two reasons why that association would be beneficial.

COMMUNICATION

> **"The quality of your life will be determined by the quality of your communication."**
>
> **— Anthony Robbins**

The ability to communicate with those around you in an effective way will set you apart as a leader. Communication is a broad subject. It could include several areas such as verbal, nonverbal, and written communication. This section will focus on how we communicate with others. Have you ever known anyone who has little or no tact with other people? They just say what they feel and evaluate their comments later. Some people are like bulls in a china shop. They damage almost everything they touch.

Top leaders develop a keen sense of awareness when they are working with others. They can read people's responses and tactfully handle every situation even if the situation is unpleasant. The following paragraphs outline several ideas on how you can develop tact and increase your communication skills.

Smile. Go ahead and smile right now. Smiling can actually change a person's attitude. After one of my workshops two young women, Jennifer and Michelle, approached me. Jennifer said, "Michelle makes

everyone around her smile. Even if you have nothing to smile about she makes you smile." I looked at Michelle to see if she would agree with Jennifer's analysis.

"Is that true?" I asked. Michelle said, "Absolutely, you are not fully dressed until you put one on." What a great statement. I turned to Jennifer and asked, "does smiling when you do not want to make you feel better?" She replied, "well, yes I guess it does." Sometimes just smiling when you don't feel like it can brighten your mood.

Smiling also gives you the appearance of being approachable. People want to be around happy, friendly people. Seldom do we strive to associate with the grumpiest person around.

Look people in the eyes. Have you ever asked someone a question and they looked at everything but you? What conclusions do you naturally draw? You may think either they lack self esteem or they are lying. Looking people in the eyes demonstrates confidence in yourself and your ideas. However, there are some cultures where looking people in the eye is a show of disrespect. Leaders seek to understand cultural differences.

Avoid proving someone wrong. If you would like to get rid of a friend or two, simply prove them wrong in front of a group of their peers. Successful leaders allow people to come to their own conclusions. When disagreeing with someone a person may say, "Well, I never thought of it that way." Then they interject their opinion by saying, "Have you ever looked at it from a different side of the issue?" Notice they are not saying "have you lost your mind? That is the dumbest, most uninformed statement I have ever heard!" If that approach is taken, what is the person on the receiving end thinking to him or herself? Probably something like, "Oh really, who do you think you are? I don't need to take this from you."

Have you ever been proven wrong by someone else? How does it make you feel? Mad? Embarrassed? Vengeful? Maybe all three.

Does proving a person wrong make a relationship stronger? No. However, asking questions forces the person you disagree with to look at the issue from a different perspective.

Recognize people's achievements. Remember the stickers of accomplishment students used to receive in elementary school? It was amazing to see the effort people would put in to earn a sticker. For some reason those little signs of achievement start to disappear as a person gets older. In our world today it

seems a person can do one hundred things right and not hear a word about it. But as soon as one mistake is made, people jump on your case. Too often great work goes unnoticed. Leaders look for ways to recognize achievement. Giving honest and sincere recognition and praise builds other people's self esteem. Keep in mind that praise is given without the intention of getting something in return. The objective is not manipulation. Honest, sincere praising in public adds more power. The more others hear about an accomplishment, the better they will feel.

Give people the benefit of the doubt. Have you ever heard a rumor and instantly believed it? Even though rumors are not confirmed fact, most people believe them. Has an untrue rumor ever been spread about you? If is has happened, you know the frustration. We may say "don't believe everything you hear." If we make that statement, we must live it. Giving people the benefit of the doubt means we reserve judgment on others until the true facts are revealed. Everyone has jumped to a conclusion that was inaccurate and then felt embarrassed when the truth was revealed. **If we want others to explore the truth before judging us, we must do the same for them.**

Think before you talk. If only communication was like a tape recorder. Any statement you made that wasn't thought about could simply be erased and started over. Unfortunately, that is not the case. Talking before you fully think out the implication of the comment can cause major damage to a relationship. Even if the words are said in jest, they can still cause resentment and anger. Leaders ask themselves several questions before speaking. Some of the questions may include "how will they perceive my comment?" or "what is the best way to tell him the idea has a few glitches?" It is impossible to read how your listeners will respond. If a person takes just a few seconds to think about their comments before stating them, the chances of wanting to erase the statement dramatically decreases.

Thinking before you talk also means a person avoids blowing their top and getting angry. Hotheads are usually poor leaders. People do not appreciate being screamed at for a mistake they made. Leaders do get mad. They just save their anger for a time when it's appropriate and express it in a manner that is constructive. **When a leader loses their cool, people should be surprised.** If leaders always yell, scream, or holler, everyone gets used to the fact they are out of control and suddenly their credibility evaporates.

Criticize with care. Magicians understand how to be careful with any trick. One trick that requires a delicate hand is piercing a balloon with a needle. It's amazing! Passing a needle though a balloon seems impossible. The needle penetrates the balloon and is retracted without the balloon being popped. Leaders use that philosophy when they criticize others. They do it carefully and gently.

When giving criticism to others it's vital to criticize the performance, not the performer. Criticism may be made with a series of questions. Remember what happens when we are out to prove someone wrong. Questioning allows people to draw their own conclusions as to how their performance could have been better. It makes them feel comfortable taking responsibility for a mistake and encourages them to improve the next time a similar situation arises.

Develop a vocabulary. The words you use create an image. If you walk around using words in an incorrect form, people draw the conclusion that you may not be all that intelligent. My seventh grade English teacher would demand a long writing assignment from any of her students who used the word "ain't." It didn't take long before that slang word disappeared from several people's vocabulary.

The last part of this chapter concentrates on self communication. **Developing a journal** allows leaders to keep a log of thoughts, events, failures, and success stories. A journal is a private set of notes that gives you the opportunity to express all your feelings. It can be filled with pictures, poems, and newspaper articles. These items can deal with your life and trends in society. The journal can  become your own history book. By recording the events and thoughts of today a person can monitor their growth personally and physically. Every one should write at least one book in their lives. A journal can be a book authored by the one and only you.

The following are general guidelines to keeping a journal.

1. Date each entry.
2. Commit to writing in the journal at least once a week.
3. Write at a variety of different times of the day and week.
4. Include pictures and articles.
5. Write your inner most thoughts and questions.
6. Keep the journal in a safe place.
7. Review the journal often to monitor growth and insight.

Those are a few practical ideas on increasing communication skills. If they are used, it's incredible to see positive new changes our relationships take on.

EXERCISE:

1. Which of the communication skills do you feel is most important? (smile, look people in the eyes, avoid proving someone wrong, recognize people's achievements, give people the benefit of the doubt, think before you talk, criticize with care, develop a vocabulary, and develop a journal) Why?

2. Have you violated any of the suggestions listed in question #1? What happened?

3. From the situation you described in question #2, if you could do it over, what would you change?

EDUCATION

One of the neighbor boys, Kevin, loves to play baseball. He is very skilled for a young man of four. As a matter of fact he told me he would be playing for the Minnesota Twins by the time he was nine. This got me excited since he promised to give me season tickets if he made the team.

One day my door bell rang and Kevin asked me to throw him a few pitches. We went to the back yard and in a short time he had me running all over chasing the balls he hit. Kevin had the ability to not only make contact but he could step into the pitch which gave him more power. Maybe the Twins could use him! After twenty minutes it was time for his sister, Elizabeth, to take a few swings.

Because she had not practiced very much, hitting the ball was more difficult for her. I pitched roughly twenty times and she missed the ball on several attempts. Unfortunately, she didn't even make contact with the ball on many pitches. Her frustration was very apparent. After watching several swings, I noticed her timing was off and she was not stepping into the pitches. To help with her swing, I physically demonstrated how to step into the pitch and told her to concentrate. We practiced this technique many times. After she felt comfortable with the swing and stepping into the pitch, we decided to practice with the ball. As the next pitch arrived, Elizabeth 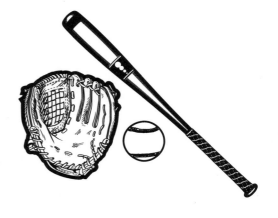 carried out all the suggestions and smacked the ball into the next door neighbor's yard. Her rhythm and swing allowed her to hit the ball solidly.

Her smile was worth a million dollars. "I did it!" she screamed. "Throw me another one, Mr. Hillier!" she exclaimed. The next pitch she hit was just the same. She ran into the house yelling, "Mom, Mom, I know how to hit. I just needed to learn how to step into it. Come out and watch me." I threw her a few more pitches and sure enough she hit every one of them with a powerful swing. It made my day to see her succeed.

I walked away from that experience thinking that **"Just learning to do one thing differently or better can increase a person's performance dramatically."** Will that one new skill be enough for the rest of her baseball career?

Absolutely not! What if she doesn't continue to educate herself and improve in the sport? Obviously, she will be in trouble. Ten years from now she may be on a high school fast pitch team. Just knowing how to step into a pitch will not be enough. She will have to learn several additional skills. In essence, she will have to continue to educate herself or her growth will be stunted.

Young leaders understand the power of education. They are never satisfied with their current level of knowledge, but they thirst to know more. They have a keen desire to constantly search for one or two additional strategies or skills that will give them an edge. If you have read this far in the book you have demonstrated the same thirst. Hopefully, you have discovered at least one or two strategies you were not aware of before reading it.

Now that we're in the 21st century, education is becoming increasingly important. Leaders understand education is like a ticket into the ball game of life.

If you have ever been to a major sporting event you understand there are several seating options. Let's use baseball for this example. As you walk into the stadium and observe the different seating options you see a variety of choices. Some people are sitting in the upper right field deck in the last row. Those seats

seem like they are a mile from home plate. As you continue to scan the stadium, you notice some people sitting on the first base side in the first row. Why do some people sit way back in right field and use binoculars to see the action, while others seated close to the field are almost in the game? There is a simple answer. The people closer to the game paid a bigger price for their ticket. Because they paid a bigger price for the ticket, the location of their seat was better. What kind of ticket will you hold when entering the ball game of life?

When you graduate from high school you will receive a "ticket" into the ball game of life. The ticket is in the form of a diploma. Some tickets are very valuable and allow you to choose any seat in the ball game of life. You can sit close to the action because you have dedicated yourself to knowing and learning as much you possibly can.

Unfortunately, some people's tickets will only allow them to sit in the last row, looking from a distance to get a glimpse of the game. They took the easy, lazy route in education. Their attitude may have been "Who cares about education? I don't need to know this junk anyway." That attitude put them in the back row of life.

There are also usually students who say, "All I need is a ticket into the ball game and then I will just con my way into a better seat when I arrive." This strategy may work a time or two. Eventually it catches up. **Success rarely is achieved through manipulation.**

Where do you want to sit in the ball game of life? Do you want to have the ability to write your own ticket and sit any where you want? If you have that desire you will commit to pushing yourself in the classroom. There are classes that may initially seem of little or no use to you. The most successful leaders find a way to make any topic relevant and useful in their lives. When it comes to selecting classes, leaders challenge themselves by taking difficult courses. They avoid taking the easy way out. Even though their grade point average may be slightly lower because of the difficulty of the class, they understand the more they stretch in the classroom, the farther they will go. **In essence, the more you know, the more you grow, the farther you go.**

The classroom is one component to education. Actual life experience is another important component. It's not enough to be "book smart." Leaders must also be street smart. They are educated in the classroom of life. There are two styles of education in life: P.E. and O.P.E. By the way, P.E. does not stand for physical education!

P.E. stands for personal experience while O.P.E. stands for other people's experience. Both kinds have their merit and importance. There are times when personal experience is the best teacher. If something positive happens, the feeling is real and personal. Chances are the feeling will never be forgotten. However, there are times when personal experience is the worst teacher. If a mistake you make causes you major pain and it could have been prevented, the pain seems even greater.

Other people's experience can be very valuable. If someone makes a major mis-

take in life, you can learn a lesson from their actions. Conversely, if someone discovers a strategy that brings them success, you can also learn a lesson worth repeating. Assume someone unlocked a secret to remembering calculus equations. Instead of beating yourself up mentally trying to memorize the equation, tap into the other person's experience and memorize the equation in the same fashion. It will probably save you an incredible amount of time and your test scores will probably improve.

O.P.E. can involve creating a relationship with a mentor. A mentor is someone who has experience or expertise in a given field. Leaders know reinventing the wheel is a silly, laborious act. If someone is achieving the results you want to achieve, seek them as a mentor. It would be smart to look for someone you look up to as a person. If they achieved success by cheating and conning other people, you may want to continue to search for someone you respect completely. When you find the right mentor, ask that person to take you under their wing and help you develop as they have developed. Most people are honored to be a mentor, provided a few rules are followed. If you are fortunate to find a mentor the first rule is to prepare, prepare, prepare. Nothing will sour a relationship quicker than showing up without a pad of paper and questions.

The second rule to mentoring is be curious without being a nuisance. Taking up too much of their time or asking questions with little relevance may cause the mentor to end the relationship. If you have four questions, ask the questions politely and move on.

The third rule is significant. Express your appreciation for your mentor's help. This means sending a thank you card, buying lunch, or making their favorite dessert for your meeting. Naive people would call this "brown-nosing." Leaders understand people want to feel appreciated. If they feel like you are not taking advantage of them and you are doing your fair share to grow as a human being, most mentors will do anything they can to help you provided you are willing to help yourself.

Mentors can also come from the written word. Thousands of people achieved incredible feats and they took the time to write out how they did it. You can learn how they reached their plateaus by reading their books. This sounds simple. You would think people would be flocking to libraries to re-

search this valuable information. Yet it has been estimated only three percent of the population has a library card. Imagine having a free treasure map sent to you that leads to the largest diamond mine in the world and passing it up because you don't have time to dig for treasure. Sounds ridiculous, doesn't it? Yet that treasure map is available to everyone at no cost and only three percent of the population has the initiative to seek out the map. I'm talking about a library card. Our libraries are filled with treasures of knowledge. Yet ninety-seven percent of the people living in the United States do not have a library card.

The strongest leaders find mentors they can work with personally and also seek other mentors' knowledge through books. The following are recommended books for achievers. I've had the opportunity to read these books and the information has impacted my life in a powerful, positive way.

Recommended Readings

1. **Playing Beyond the Scoreboard – A team captain's guide to a season of significance** by Craig Hillier *
2. **Lead Now or Step Aside** by America's Top Youth Speakers, ChesPress Publications *
3. **Yogowypi Factor** by Bill Cordes *
4. **How to Win Friends and Influence People** by Dale Carnegie
5. **The 7 Habits of Highly Effective Teens** by Stephen Covey
6. **Awaken the Giant Within** by Anthony Robbins
7. **See You at the Top** by Zig Ziglar
8. **The Magic of Believing** by Claude Bristol
9. **Developing the Leader Within You** by John Maxwell
10. **Bringing Out the Best in People** by Alan Loy McGinnis

* Book available through Winning Edge Seminars

Mentoring shortens your learning curve. **Success Leaves A Pattern!** If you really want to achieve as a leader, follow the path other leaders have paved. After you have grown to a certain level, begin to pave your own way and eventually be willing to share your own pool of knowledge.

Education will give you a major advantage in life. It is the one thing that can't be taken away. By using personal experience and other people's experience appropriately, you can literally write your own ticket into the ball game of life.

EXERCISE:

1. Get a library card.

2. Read or listen to a resource that will help you grow.

3. Seek out a mentor and write down three questions you would like to ask this person. If possible, set up a meeting with this person to discuss those questions.

VISUALIZATION

Imagine a plane full of passengers. The airplane captain starts to speak to the passengers on the intercom by saying "Thank you for choosing our airline. I'm not exactly sure when we'll take off or when we'll arrive. As a matter of fact, I'm not even sure where we're going. Hopefully, we'll get to where you want to go at the right time. For now, just sit back and enjoy the journey."

You say, "that's the dumbest thing I've ever heard. A captain not knowing where they're going? Never!" Yet how many people who are captains of their own life journey have no idea where they are going or how they will get there? One thing is for certain. If a person does not have a plan, destination, or target, they will surely end up somewhere that they don't want to be.

Are you willing to do that? Are you willing to let your future be determined by chance or circumstance? Or do you want to learn how to have the ability to influence your future? Let's face it. It is impossible to totally control your future, but you do have some say as to what you can achieve in your life.

Most people have been told "you have to set goals." According to a Harvard study, 97% of our population has no written concrete goals. No plan. Most people are just crossing their fingers and hoping it will all work out in the end. They believe hard work is enough. I've got news for you. Hard work is only part of the program.

You can go to work, get excited, and get off the ground but if you do not know where your final destination is you will end up landing in foreign territory. However, if you will develop the skills of an airplane pilot you will not only be able to plan your destination, you will arrive in an effective, efficient manner. Goal setting will help you set a flight plan for your life's accomplishments.

The word **GOALS** can be used as an acronym. Each letter in the word "goals" stand for a strategy that can be used. If you will consider each of these letters as you are determining a personal flight plan, the goals and your achievements will be incredible.

The **G** stands for **GENUINE.** A goal must be something you have a genuine passion for. In other words, if bicycling is not fun or interesting to you, setting a goal to bicycle across the United States is not a genuine goal. It's of little or no interest to you so setting a goal like that will be of no benefit. If you are going to set a goal you have to really want it and be willing to work for it. If you really want it, amazing opportunities and events will suddenly just pop up out of the blue.

Many people have ideas about goal setting. Some say be realistic; others say be idealistic. It seems the "istic" part is right. Sometimes being realistic does not challenge you and idealistic is usually unattainable. Falling short of an idealistic goal leads to frustration. I believe the best "istic" starts with the letter O. The **O** in Goals is **OPTIMISTIC**. In other words, set a goal that is better than your best but still attainable. Optimistic goals will challenge you to work hard. Realistic goals indicate average work with little challenge. It is tempting to set realistic goals because many people have the idea they are easier to achieve. That may be true. The problem is that realistic goal setting sometimes causes individuals to sell themselves short of reaching their true potential.

Let's examine this with a physical demonstration. If it is feasible, stand up. Place your feet shoulder width apart. Keeping your feet firmly planted on the floor, take your right hand and raise it as high as you can in the air. Hold it for a second. Now raise it higher. Hold it for three seconds. Now raise it even higher. And hold it for two seconds. Now put your hand down. Interesting. The first time you raised your hand you probably thought it was raised as high as possible until you were instructed to go higher. Then you thought you maxed out.

"Even higher," you were instructed. It probably amazed you that it was possible to go further on three different occasions. Why were you asked to do that? It was not to make your right arm longer then your left. It was to show that when you think you cannot go any farther, you can. You can stretch and accomplish even more. That is what setting optimistic goals means. Set goals so they are better than your best and yet achievable if you stretch. It is difficult to set optimistic goals in a world that is developing an attitude of "good enough." Too many people adopt the attitude of doing the least they can do to get by. Academically speaking, the attitude is that "C's will get you a degree. The grade doesn't matter as long as you pass." That attitude will not cut it any more. It's one thing to get a C if that is the best you can possibly do. However, if you achieve a C in a class and you could have optimistically achieved a B with a proper plan, you have just sold yourself short of achieving your potential. Achieving is not about being better than someone else; it's trying to be better than you can be or have been. That may sound like an advertisement, but it is so true. Economically speaking, only putting 70% effort in your job, generally leads to unemployment. Can you imagine if your employer paid you just 70% of your salary to match your effort output? Maximum effort equals maximum results.

If you've set optimistic goals you must also have the A in goals. And the **A** is **ACCURATE**. Exactly what do you want and exactly how will you achieve it? When I present an in-person session on goal setting, I challenge a group to set an academic goal for the year. I frequently hear "I'm going to get better grades." "When?" is my first question. "This quarter? Next quarter? Next year? When?" Just stating "I am going to get better grades" is far from being accurate. Assume a student responds with "next quarter." My next question is, "Great, how are you going to get better grades?" The standard answer usually is, "by working harder." "How *specifically*?" is my next question. This is followed by a student response of "I'll spend more time on each subject." All of these responses are good, but they are also very general. In the airplane example, pilots know exactly when they are to leave,  how many air miles they need to fly, and how much fuel they will need. Does that plan always work out exactly? Of course not. Various events come up:

storms, wind patterns, foggy weather. But one thing stays consistent: the goal or outcome. They are very accurate about their destination. A more accurate plan to achieve better grades would be to take a look at each subject's current grade and then set a genuine, accurate, optimistic goal for the next quarter's grade in each subject. Now the destination is set; you know where you want to be. The next part of achieving the goal is to incorporate the L in goal.

The **L** stands for **LIST**. A list details what you are striving for and describes a plan for achieving it. If someone is genuinely committed to improving academically, they will have to construct a list describing how they will attain the optimistic goal. As in the illustration mentioned earlier, a person may want to improve an English grade from a B- to an A-. That is the destination. The list becomes the

accurate flight plan. The list defines the step by step process of a flight plan. The list should be prioritized. The first item on the list should be the most important. The list may include visiting a peer tutor, getting to school 15 minutes early to go over any questions with the English instructor, spending 30 minutes every night on homework, turning assignments in on time, asking questions in class, viewing a study skills video tape, taking accurate notes, or sitting in the front of the class. All these items will go on a list which in essence becomes your personal recipe for success. If you follow the recipe, you will achieve the desired results.

This list should be visible. The 3X5 recipe card method is very effective for setting goals. The plain side of the index card should state the optimistic goal. It may say, THE SECOND QUARTER OF THIS YEAR I WILL ACHIEVE AN A- IN ENGLISH COMPOSITION. It is important to state the goal in positive terms. Successful goal setters determine what they do want versus what they don't want. The reason behind this idea stems from how the subconscious mind operates. The subconscious mind does not understand a negative goal. For example, a person may set the following goal. "STARTING IMMEDIATELY-I AM NOT GOING TO SLEEP PAST SEVEN A.M." The subconscious mind does not comprehend the word "not." It simply hears, "STARTING IMMEDIATELY- I AM GOING TO SLEEP PAST SEVEN A.M."

This may sound confusing. Try this example. Whatever you do right now, do not think of an elephant with huge tusks. Do not think about how massive an elephant with a tusk can be. Remember, think of anything but an elephant.

What did you think of? The vast majority of people say they thought of or pictured an elephant even though they were instructed not to. Why? The subconscious mind does not understand negative language.

Instead of stating, "I AM NOT GOING TO SLEEP PAST SEVEN A.M., the statement should say, "STARTING IMMEDIATELY, I AWAKE EVERY MORNING AT OR BEFORE SEVEN A.M. FEELING REFRESHED AND READY FOR THE DAY." That statement will literally program the subconscious mind to wake the body up at seven a.m. If you doubt this, think about a time when you knew you had to awake early in the morning for something extremely important. You may have told yourself to wake up at a certain time. Chances are you woke up at exactly that time or a few minutes prior to the alarm going off. The subconscious mind has an amazing power. It is constantly working. Now it can be working more effectively with you. The subconscious mind will become even more valuable if the S in goal setting is used properly.

The **S** in goals stands for **SYMBOLS**. Symbols are pictures or statements that are constantly visible and have meaning for the goal. If improving grades is the goal, I would suggest you design a report card that looks exactly like the school's report cards. By the way, this is not for you to put all A's on and show your parents or to impress your friends. It is to help you actually see the intended results.

Every day of our lives we are flooded with advertising. We see it on billboards, newspapers and magazines, hear it on the radio, and view it on television. The more a product or service is advertised the greater the chance a person will buy. I'm suggesting we use the power of advertising to our benefit. We can, in essence, advertise in our own mind. The more we flash the desired result in our minds, the greater the chance we will achieve the goal.

Symbols are an advertisement for the subconscious mind. The advertisements allow the subconscious mind to go to work on the goal. The fascinating thing about the subconscious mind is it does not know the difference between a fact and a fantasy. Have you ever had a terrible nightmare and woke up scared to death? If you have, the subconscious mind is responsible for those feelings. If you can get the subconscious mind to go to work, you have developed an edge. It is almost like an auto pilot. It will help guide you to your desired destination. You still have to do a majority of the work, but it is comforting to know you have this powerful tool available.

The sample report card should illustrate the optimistic grades. When a person looks at the card, it's as if the goal has already been achieved. Another symbol could be a picture of a young person studying or your name printed on the dean's list. There are hundreds of symbols a person can use. The key to symbols is to make them visible. The sample report card could be on your bathroom mirror. The studying picture could go above a desk at home. The mock honor roll list could go inside of a locker. If the goal is to improve overall grade point average, write that number out on several cards and place one on the visor in your car if you drive or put one in your wallet or purse, anywhere that you will see it multiple times. The more you see it the better off you are. Suddenly, the subconscious mind will take over. Sticking to the list will start to become natural versus a chore.

Disclaimer! If you set the goals without considering the G or the genuine in goals, it is likely they will not be achieved. If you do not have a genuine interest in accomplishing the goal, the O-A-L-S are just a waste of time and effort. The old phrase, "you can lead a horse to water but you cannot make it drink" is true. No one can force you to set and reach goals but you. All of us at one time or another have been sold on someone else's goal. If it's not your goal it seems like it's not worth the effort to achieve the goal.

GENUINE-OPTIMISTIC-ACCURATE-LISTED-SYMBOLS

Those are the five guidelines for goal setting. The great part of this system is those strategies will work in all areas of goal setting. Many people ask, "In what areas of my life should I set goals?" There is no pat answer to that question. It is important to set goals in as many areas in your life as you want to improve. These areas could be general enough to include physical fitness, academic or athletic performance, relationships, spiritual growth, your health, or giving back to your school or community as we discussed in the chapter on contribution. In short, any part of your life that you want to improve is a place to set goals.

Most leaders have immediate goals that can be accomplished within fourteen days. Short term goals usually follow a two week to six month time line. Long term goals are from six months to several years.

One final thought on goal setting. It is an ongoing, never ending process. After you have accomplished one goal, start on another goal card. The next step is to set another goal to replace the goal that was achieved. **Stretch!** Never be totally satisfied with where you are at—always be in motion. If you use the 3X5 card method, consider keeping those cards as a demonstration of what you have accomplished. There may come a day when you get down on your self. Reviewing the goals that have been accomplished will normally give you a boost and the enthusiasm you need to continue to work on achieving the new goal you have set.

Plotting a map of success dramatically increases the odds of reaching your potential. Remember, goals must be written down. It is very important to take action right now and set a goal in the following chapter exercise.

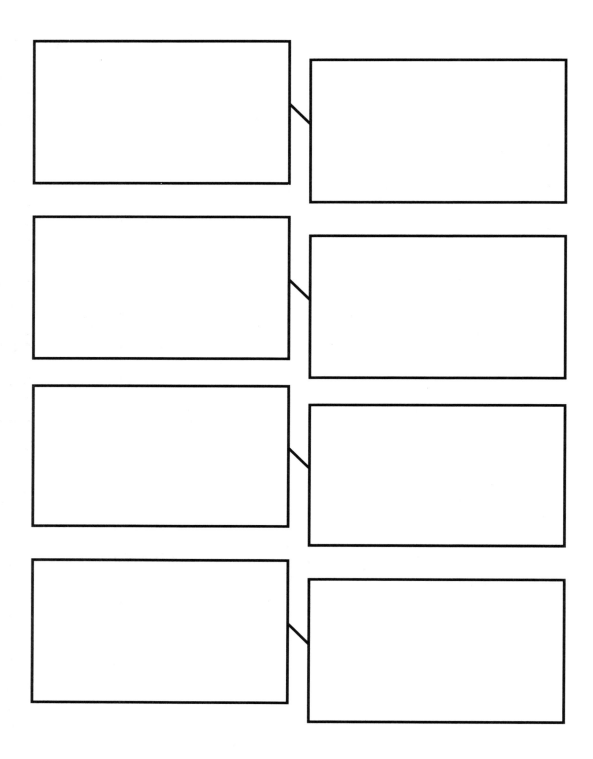

EXERCISE:

Below is the example I used in the chapter about improving an English composition grade. Using the 3 X 5 card method, I stated the positive goal on the card's blank side and the "flight plan" or list of how I want to achieve that goal on the card's other side. In the blank boxes, please plan your goals. When you are finished, transfer the information to real 3 X 5 cards, gather various symbols as reminders of your goal and put them wherever they are most visible to you. Good Luck!

The second quarter of this year
I will achieve an A- in
English composition.

1. Visit a peer tutor.
2. Get to school 15 minutes early to talk with the teacher.
3. Devote 30 extra minutes for English homework.
4. Turn in assignments on time.
5. Check out study skills tape in library.

MOTIVATION

Motivation is a mystery. There is a fallacy about motivation. Some people believe motivation involves jumping up and down, screaming and hollering. That's not motivation. That's insanity.

Motivation is creating a sense of excitement inside that is expressed on the outside. The fascinating fact about motivation is that what excites or motivates one person may not motivate another. Every individual is motivated differently. Some people are motivated to have money or power while others, such as Mother Teresa, are motivated to live a life of poverty and achieve world peace. Certain individuals are motivated to be happy while others are motivated by inflicting pain on others. Hitler would be a prime example of someone who was motivated by creating pain in people's lives.

According to author, speaker, and consultant Anthony Robbins, "People are motivated one of two ways: to seek pleasure or to avoid pain." As simplistic as that sounds, it's accurate.

Think about a term paper assignment. The instructor gives the assignment; each student has one month to complete the paper. It's interesting to observe how different people accomplish this task. Some people do absolutely nothing the first two weeks. They do not even think about the subject of the paper. In the same two weeks other students are motivated enough to have the first draft finished. Why would one student have the paper almost done while the other has not even thought of a subject?

There could be several reasons. The person who has not started the paper believes it would be more painful to start the project now than to go out with a group of friends to have fun. The person who has it nearly finished believes there will be more pleasure in their life if the project is complete. That way when they go out with a group of friends their attitude will be more relaxed because they won't have to worry about that rotten paper.

When will the procrastinator start on the paper? As soon as there is more pain in not doing the paper than in doing it. When the worrying thoughts of an "F" override the pleasure of putting it off, the pen starts to hit the paper.

Are you more motivated to avoid pain or seek pleasure? The answer may vary according to the circumstance. There may be time when achieving an "A" in a class would create a tremendous amount of pleasure and pride. However, a student requiring a certain grade point average to qualify for an athletic team or scholarship feels an incredible amount of pain if the grade is not attained. The desired result is the same. How a person attempts to achieve it will vary from person to person.

The pain versus pleasure principle is valuable when working with others. The key element to remember is that people are motivated differently. Leaders can mistakenly try to motivate others the way they themselves want to be motivated. Instead, effective leaders learn a variety of ways to motivate others.

The pain and pleasure principle is a major piece of the motivational puzzle. There are a few other pieces that help leaders complete the puzzle. Becoming a motivated person does not just happen without thought and practice. Motivated people use several strategies to stay excited and passionate no matter what the circumstances. It seems most people let events shape their enthusiasm and attitude. Motivated people create the feeling inside and then express it on the outside. The following ideas will help successful leaders to stay fired up without burning out.

Become proactive or reactive?

There are some people who let outside circumstances determine their attitude. If the weather is bad, they decide their attitude will be the same. If the team they are on is having a winning season, they are happy-go-lucky. If the team is on a losing streak, they are down in the dumps. Proactive people are those rare individuals who make a decision that they will decide on their attitude. No matter how bad the situation is, they look for the silver lining. If the team has been losing, they don't enter a game thinking, "we will probably lose this one too." Rather, they enter the game thinking, "we haven't been playing too well up to this point, but today is a brand new day and if we execute our game plan we can win." The impact of becoming proactive is immense. Proactive people decide their attitude while reactive people seem to drift down the river of life. They do not have a rudder to steer them to their desired location. Remember, ultimately you are the one who is in charge of your thoughts and actions.

Watch what you watch. If a person views the first ten minutes of any newscast they will probably see a variety of murders, robberies, and other violent acts. It is difficult to stay fired up and be happy when you see someone has just been killed in a drive-by shooting. By being careful with what you watch, you can be up on current events, but still keep a healthy perspective. However, leaders understand that being exposed to this negative information will have an impact on their attitude. Positive leaders can tune into a newscast and watch good and bad news knowing they can learn from both bits of information and not let the bad news cloud their attitude.

Listening or viewing positive messages is another tactic leaders use to stay fired up. Most libraries have several audio and video tapes available from authors like Zig Ziglar, Anthony Robbins, Bobee Gee, Denis Waitley, Lilian Glass, Florence Littauer, Stephen Covey, or Brian Tracy. The men and women who present these messages share countless ideas on creating and maintaining motivation. A daily diet of motivation from an audio or video program can be an excellent start to a leader's day.

In addition to audio and video programs, leaders surround themselves with positive messages on posters, calendars and pictures. The visual reminders help a person stay excited and on task.

Creating an oxygen tent that keeps out negativity is another powerful strategy motivated leaders use. When a person is very ill an oxygen tent is placed around them to provide clean air and keep out any germs or diseases that could potentially be harmful. Even though a person can see out of the tent it protects them. Effective leaders create an imaginary oxygen tent around themselves. If a negative person is trying to disarm a leader by gossiping or criticizing someone in a group, the imaginary tent prevents the negativity from permeating to the leader's attitude. It is difficult to keep the oxygen tent strong as others will continue to try and poke holes through it. Positive leaders find a way to mentally repair the damage immediately.

Setting optimistic goals is another way to maintain a person's motivation. As we discussed in the visualization chapter which covered goal setting, optimistic goals are set at better than your best, yet are attainable. When a person has a goal that will stretch them physically and mentally, motivation is increased. **Working toward optimistic goals will create the emotion of motivation.** Setting low or no goals causes laziness. The more activities a person has going, the more motivated they will be. It is important to set a reasonable deadline for the completion of a goal. For example, if a person has a goal of getting into excellent physical condition within the next three years, they probably procrastinate and not even start on the goal. On the other side, setting a goal to get into top, physical shape in one week is an unreasonable deadline. It is impossible to go twenty-four hours a day. Attempting that lifestyle will cause anyone to burn out.

In addition to the goals, a person with a daily "to do" list will have little problem getting out of bed and starting the daily activities. If there is no reason to get out of bed, chances are a person will not. That is why many retired people soon die after retirement. It is not age that causes their passing but often lack of anything to do with their time. Leaders live to achieve by doing something productive every single day.

Motivated leaders get up early! A person can get an incredible amount done if the day is started out early. If a person committed to getting up just thirty minutes earlier than they do right now their entire life could change. It has been proven the first half hour of a person's day has a major impact on how the rest of the day will go. So often people sleep until the last possible moment, rush to the shower, and grab a bite to eat on their way out the door to school or work. When they arrive they feel like they are in a hurry and their mind still is not working properly.

Effective leaders get up early and feed their brain before the rest of the day begins. Earlier in the chapter the subject of a daily diet of motivation was covered. If a person spends a half hour each day, five days a week exposing themselves to powerful, positive information, their lives and the lives of those around them will improve dramatically. Trying to listen to tapes or read after a long day is better than not doing it at all, but typically fatigue sets in and it is easy to put reading or listening aside until the next day. The most successful people start their day off right with a half hour of educational nourishment. Developing this habit will give anyone who uses it a major advantage in life.

Listen to upbeat music! Have you ever been completely exhausted and some upbeat music suddenly started playing? Maybe you starting singing with the group or acting like an orchestra conductor directing the music or maybe you started dancing to the music. After the song was over or turned off how did you feel? Usually energized. You forgot you were tired and started whatever you were working on. It's amazing the impact music has on the human mind and body. It can be like an energy pill.

Professional sports teams often use powerful, loud, and upbeat music to get the crowd excited. The music is played during introductions and break time. The song usually gets people to cheer, clap, or sing. The music creates emotion.

To test this example, think of the song "Jingle Bells." Actually hum this song to yourself. What do you think of? You probably answered Christmas. Why? The song is associated with the Christmas holiday. What happens when you hear a trumpet play "Taps"? A person might think about death or the military.

Have you ever heard a song from years ago and thought about a person or a certain situation? The brain responds to the music by remembering an event or feeling tied to the song. Leaders understand that positive, uplifting music can create a feeling of motivation with an individual or with a group.

The final strategy to staying motivated is to have fun. No matter what you are doing, find a way to involve fun. To work all the time and not kick back for a good time is the life of a fool. Leading should not be a chore. Motivated leaders create a fun atmosphere by learning to laugh.

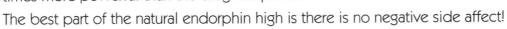

Laughter actually creates a natural high. Scientists have proven that when a person laughs, natural chemicals called endorphins are released into the blood stream. Endorphins are three hundred times more powerful than the drug morphine. The best part of the natural endorphin high is there is no negative side affect!

By following the strategies of motivation, others will soon catch a spark from you and get fired up to make a difference. Because you are in a motivated state of mind it is crucial to complete the chapter exercise. Finishing the exercise right now will create an incredible amount of pride in yourself because it demonstrates self discipline and motivation. By procrastinating, putting the exercise off until a better time, you may be missing out on a valuable tool that can create a change in your life.

EXERCISE:

1. When you are motivated, what are your surroundings like (music, friends, activities)?

2. When you are unmotivated, what are your surroundings like?

3. What would life be like if you were reactive versus proactive?

4. Get up thirty minutes earlier tomorrow and do an activity that is motivating for you and see how the rest of your day goes.

ORGANIZATION

One challenge leaders face is keeping everything organized. Young leaders are very busy people. Some young people go to school everyday, have responsibilities around home, participate in extra curricular activities, get involved in community service, hold down a part time job, and have relationships with friends and family in addition to being a part of a leadership team. All of this can be frightening if they are not organized.

Have you ever missed an assignment or club meeting because you forgot about it? Have you ever lost an important phone number because the scrap of paper it was written on disappeared? Have you ever put something down in your room and couldn't find it two minutes later? Have you ever had so many things to do that you didn't get anything done? If this has happened, you know the frustration of not being organized.

Becoming organized allows a person to get twice as much done in the same time. Because they recorded the location in their planner, organized people are not running all over the place looking for the meeting site. Seldom do organized leaders miss an assignment because they did not know when it was due.

Organization is an important ongoing process that allows you to continue a busy life style. Getting organized is not always easy but the cost of being unorganized is immense. If this skill is mastered, a person will also have more leisure time because they completed all the daily requirements in a shorter period of time.

That does not mean you have to invest in a huge day time planner that would fill a locker or two. To get organized you'll need a monthly calendar and a note pad. The size of each of these depends on your needs. It is convenient if the two components are connected or bound. Some students three hole punch a calendar and some typing paper and place it in a three ring binder. This system is inexpensive and very flexible. The *Month At A Glance* or *Day Runner* time manager is similar to this format. They can be purchased for three to four dollars at a book or office supply store. Some students prefer a palm pilot. If that fits you, go for it.

The calendar is an excellent overview for test dates, extra curricular events, club meetings and various other appointments. A full year calendar allows a person to project deadlines months from the day they are set. Using a pencil to write in the journal may be beneficial as plans and dates do change. It's easier and neater to erase a mistake or change something versus scratching the change out with a pen.

The note pad serves several purposes. It can be divided into several sections which may include brainstorming new ideas, recording notes from an organization meeting, or compiling a "to do" list. The blank pad allows a person to produce a custom day planner.

The "to do" list is a crucial part of getting organized. A prioritized list will save an incredible amount of time and energy. Most time management experts suggest keeping a running list of responsibilities to be handled within twenty-four to forty-eight hours.

The list can be compiled by first glancing at the large calendar. If a person sees a math test approaching in two days, studying for it will probably be a part of the list. Viewing the overall calendar may produce a list of twenty things to do, or it may mean concentrating on just one task.

While compiling the list it is not important to prioritize immediately. The key is to record all of the responsibilities. Prioritizing will take place after the list is complete. It is important to date the list as you will retain the list for future reference.

How many things should be on the list? Too many items usually leads to frustration; too few leads to laziness. There is not a pat answer because it depends on the day or week.

The best time to compile a "to-do" list is the night before. If this is done, the subconscious mind starts to work on the items on the list as you sleep. Have you ever concentrated to remember a fact, but it didn't come to your mind? Maybe it was on the tip of your tongue but it couldn't come out. Then you went to sleep and upon waking up the answer was there? If this has happened to you, the subconscious mind took over and searched the file cabinets of your mind to find the answer. By compiling a list of facts or "to do" items the evening before, an answer to a problem or creative idea that you have been working on can suddenly becomes evident. Having the list ready also helps you save time as you won't have to take the time to develop it in the morning.

After the list is compiled, prioritizing takes place. Each item on the list can be placed in one of three categories: A, B or C.

"A" stands for important and urgent.
Example: an English essay due tomorrow.

"B" stands for important but not urgent.
Example: a research paper due in three weeks.

"C" stands for neither urgent nor immediate.
Example: an optional extra credit assignment.

Start by prioritizing the immediate and urgent items. Next to the most urgent and important item write an A-1. This indicates it's the first and most important item to be accomplished on the list. By the way, it may be beneficial to identify those items you least want to do and perhaps have been putting off several times. If you do those items first, the rest of the list looks simple. The second most important and urgent item will have an A-2 written next to it. Continue through the list categorizing all the items that fit into the A list.

The remaining list can be prioritized using the B's and C's. After this list is categorized and prioritized, you have a game plan for the day. Crossing out each item as it is completed gives a person a sense of accomplishment and the momentum to continue. At the end of the day there may be a few items on the list that were not accomplished. Those items can go on the list for the next day.

Getting organized takes some time initially. After it becomes a habit you will impress yourself and those around you with how much can be done in a short period of time without frustration. Failure to organize could cause confusion, frustration, and embarrassment.

EXERCISE:

Check off each task after it has been accomplished.

1. Obtain a year calendar.

2. Record all the important upcoming events you intend to participate in.

3. Obtain a note book.

4. Divide it into as many sections as you see necessary.

5. Write a "to do" list for tomorrow.

6. Prioritize the list.

7. Take action on the list.

DETERMINATION

Remember when you were a child and you saw something in a store you really wanted? You had to have it. You couldn't live without it. You thought about it day and night. The money you needed wasn't in your piggy bank. Stealing the money was out of the question and none of your friends had any money, so borrowing it would not work either. You begged your parents and they told you to raise the money yourself.

What happened? It depended upon how much you wanted the item. If it was a must, you started to get creative. Maybe you started doing odd jobs for your parents or for the neighbors. Mowing someone else's lawn would usually be out of the question, but since they were willing to pay you to do it, you decided it wasn't so bad after all. On hot days, the lemonade stand provided a few extra dollars. Selling a few items also helped.

Finally, the magical day arrived. You raised all the money you needed for this thing you were thinking about nonstop. Remember the feeling of pride you had when you walked into the store to actually purchase the item instead of just looking at it? Most people admit to taking better care of the items they purchase with their own money. If something is just given to you without any effort on your side, the item can be taken for granted. It seems if you pay the price, whether it is in the form of money or effort, achieving the goal means more than if it was accomplished with little effort.

Accomplishing something of value is never easy.

So often people quit when an obstacle gets in the way of achieving a goal. Some people think there is only one way to get to the goal and if their approach isn't working, they quit instead of looking at things from a different perspective.

If the vision is strong, sticking to a plan is simple. However, if the vision is not important, it is easy to quit when an obstacle presents itself.

Anyone who has accomplished something of value has paid a price. Their determination leads the way to accomplishing the goal. The following five people demonstrated the power of determination.

The first two people who have demonstrated determination are Olympic speed skaters. Just making the Olympic team shows determination. Dan Jansen entered his third Winter Olympics in 1994 without even having earned a medal. The experts said he was past his prime. Throughout his career he had been known to fall or trip during the medal race. In the 1994 Olympics, Dan made it to the finals of the 500 meter race. He was the favorite to win the gold medal. On one of the last turns of the race, he slipped just as the experts predicted. He wouldn't win the gold medal.

He had just one more race to compete in—the 1000 meters. The 1000 meters was a race he didn't even care for. Dan Jansen could have done the easy thing and quit. However, Dan Jansen is a champion. He entered the race with a determined attitude. He was willing to put all his efforts on the line. The rest of the story is history. Not only did he win the race and earn a gold medal, he set a world record.

Contrary to Dan Jansen's story is the life of another speed skater named Bonnie Blair. Bonnie Blair had been a successful racer. She entered the same two Olympics Dan Jansen had but came away with different results. In each of her two Olympics, she skated away with a gold medal. But that wasn't enough for her. She was determined to do something even more remarkable. She entered her third Olympics and accomplished something no other woman has ever done. She won three gold medals in the same event in three different Olympics. Both athletes persisted through some tough times. They were never satisfied with their current accomplishments. They constantly strived for more.

Another example of a determined individual is a young woman named Heather Whitestone. Heather Whitestone was crowned Miss America in 1994. She was the first person to win the Miss America contest with a legal handicap. She lost her hearing early on in life, but that didn't stop her. She was determined to turn her disability into an advantage. Other people thought it could not be done. Heather simply accepted her handicap and focused in on her talents, which amazed the Miss America judges. She is an inspiration to anyone who thinks they can't accomplish something because of a handicap they might have.

All of the examples up to this point have included famous people. The next person may be an ordinary individual, but he has accomplished something extraordinary. His name is Jason Bell. He graduated from high school in 1994. He had an amazing educational career. At times his life journey was bumpy. The challenge started at the end of first grade. Jason's reading teacher had beenworking with him on developing his reading skills. After a lot of work there was very little progress. Despite his effort, Jason had completed just one of the three books required to pass the first grade. Trying to determine the problem, the teacher decided to have a few tests done. Upon completing the tests, the doctors diagnosed him with ADD. ADD stands for Attention Deficit Disorder. A person with ADD has a difficult time concentrating. Concentration spans can be as short as thirty seconds. Therefore, reading a book is very challenging. After the diagnosis, a drug called Ritalin was prescribed in addition to some mental exercises. To make a long story short, Jason Bell graduated in the top twenty-five percent of his class and received a scholarship for $12,500. He used that money to attend a school that specialized in the training of emergency medical technicians. Upon graduation, Jason will be trained to ride on an ambulance crew in emergency situations.

After hearing he had ADD in first grade, Jason could have given up but he is a rare individual. He took the potential set back of ADD and transformed it into a comeback. His determination is something everyone can learn from.

The last person who has shown success is you. That's right—you! If you have read this far in the book, you are a determined leadership student. It has been estimated that only ten percent of the books checked out of a library or bought in a bookstore are read cover to cover. If you are reading this sentence you are in the top ten percent of the population.

Take a minute to think about your life up to this point. Has there been a time when you wanted to quit something, but you chose to hang in there and persist until you reached your goal? How did that make you feel? If you persisted through some challenging obstacles, you probably feel a sense of pride and confidence for accomplishing the task.

By continuing in the face of adversity, you have demonstrated you have what it takes to become an effective leader. There are going to be days when quitting looks like the only option. It may seem your vision is impossible to accomplish. Maybe the people who promised to help you are no longer there. What will you do? The true leader doesn't give up when times get tough. As a matter of fact, of the leaders I know, when the day has gone bad or the event they were planning looks like it is going to fall apart, some scream a four letter word. Before you turn the page, brace yourself—you may be surprised to see **this** four letter word.

NEXT

That's right, next. When the project fails or the grade on the paper isn't what you expected, simply say "next." By focusing on the next project or the next paper you are looking at the future instead of dwelling on the past. The only time a person really fails is if they make a mistake and don't learn from it. Mistakes are merely feedback because you learned a way that it didn't work. Successful leaders learn from their mistakes and then apply their knowledge to the NEXT situation.

Leaders use the same approach doctors take. Assume you get sick and you are waiting in the waiting room at the clinic. A person is called into the doctor's office and a few minutes later that person dies. What does the doctor do? They don't quit. They call the next person in. What if that person dies? The doctor doesn't take the rest of the day off because it's not going very well. They will probably open the door and say, "next." I am not saying that doctors are not compassionate with their patients. Doctors understand that they can not let what happened to their previous patients dictate their service with the next patient. Just like doctors, leaders need to be resilient from situation to situation.

When you find yourself wanting to quit, simply say NEXT and look at things from a new perspective. Chances are you will find a solution you wouldn't have found without facing the problem head on.

EXERCISE:

1. Review your exercises in this book and decide which skill or philosophy you are going to work on.

2. Write or email me a letter and tell me how this book helped you.

   Craig Hillier
   Winning Edge Seminars
   20712 Jutland Pace
   Lakeville, MN 55044
   e-mail: craig@craighillier.com
   www.craighillier.com

3. Describe a time in your life when you felt like you failed.

   What lessons did you learn?

   How could you use these lessons in the future?

CONCLUSION

Well, you made it! If you've read through this book you have probably decided it's time to step up as a teen leader. Hopefully the material in the book has shown you it is possible to be a leader and still keep your friendships strong.

There is just one final thought I would ask you to think about. Jim Rohn challenged me with four questions to ponder. As we conclude, I would like you to think about these questions.

WHY?

Why try this hard? Why get up early and stay up late trying to make a difference? The best answer to that question is another question.

WHY NOT?

Why not see what you can do? You've got the tools to make it happen. Why not put them to work?

WHY NOT YOU?

Sure it's easy to look at others and say they should be leaders because they have all the talent and skills. The exercises in the book should have shown you that the talent and skills you need to be an effective leader are at your finger tips. It's time to use them!

WHY NOT NOW?

There is no time like the present to get started. What could you do starting today to make a contribution to your school, work or community? Get the idea, get the right people around you, and then get going!

What's Next?

 If you liked this book and want to read others like it, go to
www.craighillier.com

 You will find additional ideas, quotes and products on how to
become your best.

 If your school or organization is looking for a fun speaker who has a
strong message, please give me a call.

I hope you enjoyed the book!

 Craig Hillier